What Critics are Saying

"This book is one of unheard passion. With each piece _____ ____, the reader gets the privilege of stepping into the freedom of Ricky's mind and soul despite the unjust detainment of his body. The poetic language of his words hit so deep that no matter if you can relate to his situation or not, you will feel them in your bones. I have had the privilege of playing Ricky Kidd in his spoken word play *Mind of the Innocent: A Spoken Word Play* in March of 2017 in Kansas City, Missouri. This was the first time I was introduced to his work, and it has changed my life ever since. From meeting him, talking with him, and bringing his text off the page, I instantly knew that what I was getting was something real, raw, truthful, honest and genuine, and not forced or manufactured. I know readers of this book, without a shadow of doubt, will discover the same."

"I came, I lived, I mattered" - Ricky Kidd

Frank Oakley III (Actor, Atlanta, GA)
Actor, Personal Trainer and Model
iSubmit Talent Agency

"Ricky Kidd's Vivid Expressions are precisely as they say. An amazing body of work that gives the world an in depth, descriptive look behind the curtain of innocence. Instead of allowing his circumstances to impact him negatively, Mr. Kidd, was able to channel that energy into something positive, producing thought provoking and emotional stirring pieces of poetry that will in no doubt, move the reader to tears and/or actions. A must read!"

Tremayne Guinn
Innocent prisoner out of Missouri

"I have spoken to Ricky many times on the phone, meaningful conversations about life, justice, family and more. I did not truly begin to feel his pain, frustration and indignation until I read "Vivid Expressions" and heard him recite his poetry. His ability to make you feel, not just understand, but really feel his emotions is immense. He has crawled out from under the collapsed building that became his life and exhibits the resilience of the human soul that demands justice of a corrupt system and offers himself as champion for those who have yet to find hope. If you read the book you will certainly feel the pure emotions of an innocent man."

Jeff Humfeld, Producer
Jaws of Justice Radio What Critics are Saying...

"Ricky is not just another case. He is not just another incarcerated man. He has a spirit. He has talents. He lives. He loves. He hurts. He is going through a struggle that so many of us will never personally endure, and he beautifully expresses all of this through his writing. This is a raw, emotional, intimate view of Ricky Kidd."

Kelsey Berkley
UMKC School of Law 2017

"Despite being wrongfully cordoned off from society for over two decades, Ricky Kidd has masterful insight into the human condition and what it means for all of us to matter as human beings. These spoken words will open your mind, pierce your heart, and free your soul, if you let them."

Sydney Ragsdale
UMKC Law Student

Vivid Expressions

A Journey Inside The Mind of The Innocent

By Ricky Kidd

Wrongfully convicted for over 20 years, Ricky Kidd, has allowed us to journey inside his mind, uncovering an array of thoughts and emotions. From sadness, to reflection, to inspiration and love. What's inside a poetic mind sent away for a crime he didn't commit? These pages will pique your interest and answer that question.

Vivid Expressions: A Journey Inside The Mind of The Innocent
© 2017 by Ricky Kidd

"Butterfly Man" Photo for Book Cover by Floyd Sampa

"Faces" Photo for Inside Cover by Floyd Sampa

Layout and Cover Design by Tribal Raine - Prysmatic Dreams Publishing

 www.PrysmaticDreamsPublishing.info

Printed in the United States of America

ISBN-13: 9781548560959

First Printing 2017

This book is dedicated to Reverend John Gray, Sr.
When I was just a boy, you gave me my first glimpse of a man...
I saw it, then sought it... Now I AM.
So glad I am... Thank You!

ACKNOWLEDGEMENTS

First and always is the acknowledgment of my personal Lord & Savior, Jesus Christ. It has totally been Him who has gotten me through. No other explanation is possible!

To my mother, Vicki Kidd, who had to first be a brave teenager and decide to give birth to me. How could I be without you? Our Mothers are the only passage to enter this world. That's a huge significance to whatever we accomplish while here.

I like to acknowledge my beautiful sister Nechelle Kidd, I often wonder if you know just how much you play a role in who I am today.

To Harriet Clark, you have been my rock through many years of massive storms. I am stronger because of you.

To Monica Gray, our love was violently ripped apart when I was wrongfully hauled away. Nonetheless, we've taken their best punch and we're still standing. Amazing! As are you.

To my amazing daughter, Infiniti Desiree Gray, I tear up as I write these expressions. Your life prevented me from taking my own. You gave me hope in my darkest hours. You were the branch at the edge of the cliff I held on to. You have been the fuel that has helped get me to this point.

To my remaining & equally amazing children, Jazmine McGill-Kidd, Austin Kidd & Raven Mitchel, your presence in my life has contributed immensely to the man I am today, simply because I know what type of father you deserve in your lives.

Jazmine, you have shown me that we can overcome the worst of storms...

Raven, you have proven that a rose can indeed grow from the concrete...

Austin, every man needs a son to pass along the jewels to put in his crown. You are a young Prince. Take yourself as such.

To Montez Woods, the first face I met in prison. Who knows what would have happened without you watching over me night after night so that I wouldn't take the easy way out?

To Floyd Sampa, my brother, true friend and partner in the vision of Humble Standards. Your artwork is from another galaxy. Thank you for letting me be a part of your genius. No one else in prison has motivated me to reach for the sky more than you. Your contribution to the dream is necessary.

Michael McRoberts, I doubt if I would still be doing poetry if it weren't for you. Your body of work inspired me to pick up where I left off. You are a true poet and a true friend.

To my most amazing & talented attorneys, Professor Sean O'Brien, Cynthia Dodge, Tricia Bushnell, my investigator - Dan Grothaus and the host of law students at UMKC School of Law working with the Midwest Innocence Project. You may not have had anything to do with the inspiration of this book, but you guys have everything to do with making sure that I regain my deserved freedom, which paves the way for other writing material the world is waiting to see. Ordinarily, food provides people with the energy needed to get through a day. As for me. I receive my energy from you all. Thank you!

So many others to thank as well, especially Sydney Ragsdale. You believed in my innocence as well as my creative ability. Thank you so much for (Mind of the Innocent). Chris Gray, Beverly Livingston, Sam Haley, Tremayne Guinn, Jeff Humfield, Courtney "Orlando" Pebbles, Debbie Dale, Anne Pless, Derek Holmes, Lamar Johnson, Denver Blackwell, Mr. Eric Ware, Mr. Matt Raymond, Ms. Regina Beggs, Mr. Rikki Rainey, Mr. Troy McCullough and if I forgot to mention anyone, which I'm sure I did, I have not forgotten your impact in my life.

You see, no one can sit down and write a piece without first having shaped his character or mind. To those mentioned above, at one point or another, that's what you have done in my life. Truth is, the impact you have left extends beyond this book. This was just a good opportunity to acknowledge you. Thank you all so very much.

PHOENIX RISING

Through these winding roads I've experienced a lot of pain
Inhaled sorrow's song deep in my soul.
I've witnessed the ungodly experience
Of being sucked into a black hole.
If my soul was a microphone you could listen
And discover the beauty of its contradictions;
Happy and sad all at the same time.
I've never been afraid to speak my mind,
Nor struggle amidst the blind.
Why are tribulations so unkind?
The down pour of rain can be so violent
Washing away a soul that was once so vibrant.
I now know what they meant when they said
I had the right to remain silent.
Once it was done they wanted me to remain silent.
Sitting at this prison desk contemplating the matter,
I'm sipping on a cup of sorrow,
Wishing it was a cup of laughter.
Wishing time could move faster.
Twenty-one years of slavery only to discover that I am the master.
Realizing there are some things I still have to master.
My vision beyond being exonerated from prison
Is to seek out wisdom that matches my vision...
Picture me as a phoenix rising
Towards a dream coming into fruition

INTRODUCTION
By Austin Bennett

Close your eyes, try to picture yourself being innocent, losing it all, life turned inside out. Imagine crying out loud, screaming at the top of your lungs but no one is hearing you. Imagine your dream vacation turning into a nightmare when you wake up and discover being left behind; all by yourself. Have you ever experienced a moment where you were telling the absolute truth, but the person didn't believe you? Take your mind back to that moment, then stretch it out for 20 years.

"Vivid Expressions" is divided into two sections. Part 1 (Then) and Part 2 (Now).

Part one includes some of my Dad's earlier writing when he first entered into the Missouri Department of Corrections. These pieces cover the years from 1997 to 2003 (age 22 to 28). It was essential, even critical for my Dad to find ways to process feelings through poetry. Part 2 consists of my Dad's most recent writings from 2013 to 2017 (age 39 to 42). There you will find a remarkable difference between the years, signifying his maturity and broadened perspective pertaining to the world as he sees it.

Whether you decide to jump into the (Now) section, begin with the (Then), or alternate between the two, what you will find along your journey is sprinkles of passion and expressions very few get to see coming from the wrongful convicted. We hope you enjoy the journey of this book as you discover what each new page has to offer.

Expressions

~THEN~ Part 1

Reflections

Family Matters

Love Words

~NOW~ Part 2

Reflections - Part 2

Family Matters - Part 2

Love Words - Part 2

1997 - 2003

~THEN~ Part 1

REFLECTIONS

What a Place to Fall Within...

What a place to fall within...
A place where the truth is very seldom
and snakism is overwhelmingly prevalent.
A place where the strong survive above all,
Yet no one is immune from the poisonous bite.
The cries of men here unheard as they clash together –
Bouncing off the concrete steel.
Old racist guards besiege you to shut up
and those who don't comply - mentally beaten
Only to cry even louder.
A place where serenity is scarce and hope is the next best thing to freedom
and dare if you will become caught without hope,
Then you live but you die...
Shattered visions torn and broke.

What a place to fall within...
A place where family is lost, futures die and tomorrows grow grim.
A place where grown men are treated like boys –
White supremacy is the color of the walls.
Some fight it, none ever win
Just a few walk away with an illusion,
While many know the countless stories untold.
A place where enemy and friend are commonly the same
Depending on the circumstances or the nature of the game.
An asylum, with no escape –
Electric fences have sealed in your fate...
What A Place to Fall Within...

Reflecting Thoughts

Ever since I've stumble into trials and tribulations
and been departed from everyone that I love;
I've come to realize that one's happiness can be snatched away
within a blink of an eye.
In this cold dark and lonely place I often find myself lying in bed at night
Staring at the ceiling wondering... Where did it all go wrong?
As each new day pass by,
I constantly find myself yearning for my love ones that I left behind
Yet they fail to acknowledge or understand the pain and difficulties
that I face in the darkest time.
There are times that I must let my thoughts and spirit travel
many miles away from here
It truly hurts me being here
but that is when I focus on the loved ones out there...
It inspires me to keep on.

A Tear Away From a Cry

From the look of my face, no one can tell the pain I hide inside.
But when I'm alone and no one is around a range of emotions begin to collide.
Trapped inside a mind that I don't want to be,
Death seems like the only way to be free.
No one can ever understand my pain – even if they tried
Even if they listened to me – even if they saw all the nights I cried
A smile that's really a frown
Shoulders & head high, but heart sunk to the ground.
Sometimes I wonder is life really just a curse
Plagued with unwanted pain since the day of my birth.
Filled with mixed emotions, I silently wonder why?
I'm realizing the depth of my pain – and I'm a tear away from a cry

Runaway Mind

I wish my mind could be free - from the violence of this cold world
I wish my mind could be free - somewhere with my three little girls

I wish my mind could be free - from all the pain in my heart
I wish my mind could be free - from loneliness cold and dark

I wish my mind could be free - in the hills of Africa somewhere
I wish my mind could be free - where peace and tranquility lives there

I wish my mind could be free - like the birds that fly above
I wish my mind could be free - from the hatred, yet filled with love

I wish my mind could be free - from the misery I see everyday
I wish my mind could be free - in any possible way.

Angel

Unbeknownst to our eyes, angels loom before our face
Heaven sent, he knows it all,
So they wait strategically placed.
Be it man or woman or even child,
it matters not the race,
We think of angels in the sky and how they fly,
but that's simply not the case.
How blessed we are to know you're there
and we marvel the thought that you even care.
Oh angel, sweet angel, you've given us hope
when it could have been lost in the wind,
You've touched our lives with a heavenly touch;
you've even become our friend.
It's not every day that we come in touch,
to look an angel in the eye,
Perhaps it's because we find ourselves,
too busy looking in the sky

A Lonely Man... A Lonely Soul,

A lonely man...
A lonely soul,
Life's infinite struggle;
Seemingly taking its toll.
Where do you run?
Where do you hide?
Stuck in this misery,
Yearning to go outside.
Disappearing dreams,
Dissipating hopes;
Shattered ambitions
A spirit that's broke.
Reaching out to touch someone
Who is not there;
Someone who does exist,
Yet, someone who doesn't care.
My tears they fall,
   My knees they shake;
A lifeless life,
   A heart that aches.
I try to be strong
   But often fall weak;
I try to hold back my tears
         But often they leak.
   Trapped in this place,
 Stuck in this hole;
         A lonely man...
A lonely soul.

Shadow of Darkness

In this darkness will light ever come...
I can't help but continue to wonder?
Will these walls ever fall like the tears in my eyes?
I'm trapped in this storm and thunder.

Dear God... Why did it happen?
Please help me understand.
Am I a part of some type of curse
or is this a part of your plan?

Wolves, tigers, serpents –
Hatred, evil and jealousy...
No place for me –
How could this be?
Stuck in this misery.

Close the casket,
Ain't I dead?
If so, then please let me rest.
Is this the grand finale?
The final chapter...
The final test?

Out of Sight, Out of Mind

If I could count the ways I feel inside, I could figure out what has caused this to happen to me and how did I end up all alone.

The strangest thing is the strangers, the ones I've met and the ones I've already known. The ones who don't know me at all and the ones who left me all alone.

It seems to me that I no longer exist- at least in the world of "The Belong".
In my time of despair, no one seems to care, as I sit here all alone.

I call for help, but no one hears my cry, my screams or even my moans.
Feeling weak when I should be strong, trying my best to hold on, as I sit here all alone

A friend in here is a knife in the back, straight through the skin to the bone.
They're a quick reminder in case you forget, that you're still left all alone.

Short and simple, my feelings, my poem – It all seems to rhyme. I can only bear witness to one conclusion... Out of sight, Out of Mind!

No, I'm Not Crazy

I yearn for a cold glass of serenity.
Or would it be warm?
Whatever it be, I could use it now!
The walls laugh at me because it sees that I am hiding my true pain.
Do I look funny hiding my true pain?
Why are the walls laughing then?
I'm saving my money to buy me an ounce of peace and tranquility.
How much does it cost anyway?
I heard that it is free, but I disagree.
Almost everything cost something.

When I wanted to be popular, it cost me a lot to dress and look nice.
When my ex-girlfriend wanted to be with me, it costed her family.
When Marvin Bynum simply wanted to respected, it cost him his life.
Everything cost!
Can somebody tell me what it will cost for an ounce of peace and tranquility?
Where is that glass of serenity... oh, here comes Anne with it now!
Thank you

Family Matters
Part 1

Kelvin Can You Hear Me, Are You Really There?

Kelvin can you hear me, are you really there? Because I need someone to talk to, I'm down in despair.

"I can hear you very clearly, but hearing me, I thought you could not. I'm surprised you even called, I thought that you forgot."

How could I forget you was a friend indeed? Full of love and laughs, but never filled with greed.

"Very kind of you to say, without nothing to gain, my feelings are mutual, I guess we both feel the same."

I think of you often and I began to smile. I have a picture of you and even your child."

"I know he's having a hard time – emotionally. I can always see him, but he can't see me."

You have a real great kid and even a great wife. I haven't seen them in a while, but I guess they are all right.

"I see what you're going through and it's a whole lot of sorrow. But you got to know one thing – there's a brighter tomorrow. "

Some say we are better off dead, I wonder if that's true. I wouldn't know, but how about you?

"I found a true peace and tranquility, but I've lost my kid and wife. Now my kid will never know his father, for the rest of his life."

Things are really different and a whole lot has changed; No more dinners, laughs and monopoly games.

"Even with that being, life still has a lot in store. I have to go right now, but we will talk later more."

Thank you for your time and you take care – Kelvin Can You Hear Me, Are You Really There?

Man to Man

An ear for listening, a shoulder to lean on
A heart for caring, a bond that is so strong.
A wave of concern, some solid support
A flow of love, an unbreakable fort.
It is you that I admire as family and friend,
A sacred relationship, among true men.
I appreciate you most for all that you do,
Whether big or small it has helped me through.
You have been in my corner for only a short time,
But the support you have given has been so divine.
I thank you brotha, in a most unique way,
and may blessings from this world be bestowed upon you this day.

Words of Concern

The sun don't always shine,
The rain don't always pour,
Life is not always pleasant
But hell, who's keeping score?
Changes in our lives can put us to the test
Challenges may be difficult,
But we have to give our best.
The darkness you may face,
You must know there is some light
A brighter day is to come,
But you must make it through the night.
People who you don't expect, oftentimes really do care,
Many miles away, still finding words to say,
That my love and concern is there.
From person to person,
From heart to heart —these words are carefully groomed,
I hope that time get much better for you
and I hope that it comes real soon.

A Little Princess Birthday

Daddy's little princess, is finally turning two
Amazed at your beauty and how fast you grew.

Very special you are to me and I wonder do you know
That your daddy really miss you and love you very so.

No words can express the way I feel in my heart,
You brought sunshine in daddy's life when it was filled with dark.

So many hidden treasures that lie within this world,
But there's no greater treasure, than daddy's little girl.

Our lives are so separate, but our ties are very close
A father who really loves you, but you don't even know

Our bond is compromised, because I can't be there
But one day you will know, just how much daddy really care.

Precious Child

Ever since I went away, I've kept you in my thoughts
Still holding on to your precious being and all the joy that you brought.

The sudden fact that we are a part eats at me everyday
Yearning so bad to be with my child, I'm fighting to find a way.

When the holiday season draws near, I cry from the bottom of my heart
Wishing that you could know that your daddy's love is so,
Even through the mist of this dark.

So many pleasures it is so, to watch your little girl grow
Yet I'm deprived of each and every moment and I don't think that you even know.

One day will bring us together – a happiness that we will come to share
A love so meaningful and so true – a joy that will feel the air.

I always like to thank God; for all that he has ever given me
And I'll always cherish the day – the day that he gave me Infiniti... Infiniti!

Precious Child (part II)

A precious child you are to me,
More precious than the treasures below the sea.

My daughter, my world, my everything,
My vision, my desire, my every dream.

Knowing that you're mine, but yet I cannot touch,
Your face, your hands and it hurts so very much.

So many nights I sit and wonder why,
Without an answer or a clue, I begin to cry.

I love you so much and you don't even know,
Who I am, where I am or will I even show.

Your life seems so fulfilled yet still so incomplete,
A father that you have yet to know, a love you have yet to meet.

As the sun set tonight and rise again tomorrow,
I hope it brings us closer together and take away all my sorrow.

Hidden Lady

She's beautiful,
She's wonderful
but very few can see...
She hides behind the rocks.
The rocks protect her,
Secure her and comforts her.
The rocks hide her from all of her worries and problems.
It is not easy for her to hide because she really want people to see her.
The rocks have become alive –
They're jealous and controlling.
People close to her tell her to come out but she continues to hide.
Some say, "You can run but you can't hide."
I say, "You can hide but you can't run."

A Present Why Not?

Off her glossy eyes Christmas lights shine,
Staring at each present wondering which one is mine?

It's all like new because she's only two,
Shining stars and lights - red, green and blue.

Filled with excitement yet seemingly sad,
Wondering to herself where is my dad?

Too young to understand too old to ignore,
Then all of sudden tears began to pour

She silently cries yearning for her father's touch,
A father she doesn't know but needs so very much.

A daughter without a father, a gift without a box,
A present not received and she wonders... Why Not?

Remember Me?

Remember me, when I was your little boy who always wanted to be under you?

Remember me, when I always talked about my dreams and desires? They were always big dreams – never less.

Remember me, as your brother who used to try and protect you from your boyfriends?

Remember me, as your brother when I got older,

How I use to try and always be there for you – never telling you no?

Remember me, who thought that I was chasing the American Dream

but really it was an illusion – a ghost?

Remember me, I was your boyfriend – the one who treated you different from all the rest?

Remember me, that one day I was so happy because you told me you were pregnant?

It can never be denied that I love you and our child.

Remember me, the times I made you all laugh – always having something funny to say?

Remember me, who was innocently hauled away to prison and I didn't understand, why me?

Remember me, I matured and did a lot of growing while locked away?

I believe that I was born in this world for the happiness of you all and didn't I accomplish that at one point or time?

One day I will face my demise – Ready or not – and no longer will I be...

"Remember Me?

Vicki

When I think back on my life as a child,
The memories that I find are truly worth the while,
All the times I was sick and needed you there,
Never letting me down, you always faithfully cared.
You taught me so much, from morals to cooking
and it is because of your genes, I turned out so good looking.
Things became bad between us, but our love always remained,
We drew our separate ways but that's one thing that never changed.
We both have been dealt some pretty bad hands,
but through the worst of it all, we still managed to stand.
Two of a kind still loving each other...
A beautiful bond between a son and his mother.
I cherish you so much and I hope you can see,
Until the day of my demise that will always and forever be.
I sent you these words because to me you are a special one,
 I love you so much...
From your one and only son.

Birthday Wishes

Twenty-seven candles lying within a cake
A very special meaning, for a very special date.
A time for reflections of the previous years that passed
Thinking to yourself... Time sure does travel fast.
You're older, much wiser and filled with a lot of life
To make it one more year that feeling must be nice.
A special thought from me to you on this special day
A special person in my heart, in such a unique way.

My Friend

A friend who's there through the most troubled times
A friend whose love is so sincere and divine.
I'm glad I have a friend who is very true
That Friend is no one else other than you.
You fulfill all my empty spaces in so many ways
I hope you continue to be around until my very last days.
I love you friend with all my heart
And I know it was love from the very first start.
I hope you value our relationship as much as I do
Because all I ever wanted I found in you.
Your smile, your laugh, your sweet soft voice
If I had to pick a new friend, you would be my only choice.
Will you promise to be mine until the very end?
My love, my flower, my queen, my friend.

Call On Me

The time will come when you will be able to conquer the unconquerable
and overcome your weaknesses and short comings.
In the midst of your adversity,
Always continue to strive and keep one foot in front of the other.
Each step you faithfully take will bring you to the very threshold of victory.
I have not counted you out! I have confidence in you
and whenever you feel weak and need someone to lean on... Call On Me

This Mother's Day

Mother you are so special to me and I hope that you understand,
I have traveled down many roads and regardless how distant you may appear,
you have always been there.
You are a mother to envy because of your special ways,
I wouldn't trade you in for nothing in the world – never in a day.
Our shortcomings and down falls we can always share together
and with the tie that binds and the love we have,
We can storm any kind of weather.
I tip my hat, take a bow and toast a drink to you
For it's your love and caring ways that has help me make it through.

This Mother's Day really mean a lot – even though I cannot be there
Your love is so true, so pure and so natural- a love beyond compare.
Take my love and words,
Cherish them and save
Keep them in a safe place,
So they will follow you to your grave.
I love you mom with all my heart and never think that I don't
With a gun to my head, one can tell me not but yet and still I won't.

As I wake up this morning
and even at night –
As I rest my head to lay
You can bet that your only son –
Is thinking of you "This Mother's Day."

Mother of All Times

It wouldn't be right for me to allow a sacred day, like Mother's Day to go by without wishing you this day – a joyful and peaceful day. Not often do we let mothers know just how much they are appreciated and if I had it my way, Mother's Day will be everyday. You have exemplified accomplishments beyond mere obligations of the average mother - A loving, caring and unique way of setting the standards for all mothers.

These are not just mere words but words from the heart. I assure you that if these words were not of truth, I wouldn't have felt so compelled to express myself in this form. If the Angels are keeping count of all the good you have committed yourself to as a mother and a grandmother – not only will the gates of heaven open for you freely, but surely you will be awarded and recognized as "Mother of All Times."

The Mother of My Child

Mother's Day has been recognized by many
and considered a special day for all mothers across the nation.
I remember when you were a child and now you are a mother
and have a child of your own.
A mother is so sacred in the eyes of all
and they deserve to be praised and appreciated.
I could not let this day go by without letting you know
that as the mother of my child,
I appreciate the responsibility that you have taken head on.
I hope that you will always continue to be that wonderful mother
that our daughter Infiniti, so well deserves.
Despite the road that our relationship has taken,
I can't help but accept the fact that you are still a mother –
The Mother of My Child.

For My Sister on Mother's Day

On Mother's Day this year, it is going to be more special than years before.
Reason why is because this year has been set aside for you as a mother,
but not only as a mother, but a very special mother.
This is the year that tally up all the sacrifices you have made,
All the responsibilities you have handled so well,
All the pain you have endured over the years
and all the love and joy you have spread among all around you.
This Mother's Day, regardless what the weatherman may say –
The sun will shine, the birds will sing, the flowers will bloom and the bells will ring
All because of you and the pledge you took as a mother is at it's high.

Not only am I proud to say how wonderful of a sister you are
but just as equally a wonderful mother.
Whether the sun shines west or the sun shines east
I hope it shines on you with love, joy and peace.

Father Time

It has come again,
The time to celebrate a day dedicated to fathers all over the world.
As I contemplate on the sacredness of Father's Day,
A specific vision of a man continues to pop in my head.
That vision is no one other than you
Yes, it's true when I say that you are in my eyes, a father to be admired.
A true definition of what I call "Father Time."
A man can stand for a lot of things in this world,
But when he can stand in recognition as one of the best fathers in time
 to another man who he did not even sire,
Then surely he must know to himself that he has reached great accomplishments.
If ever asked who is considered "Father Time" that I know in this world -
It is you, that I say...
and I say it from the essence of my heart.

Love Words

Part 1

My Heart

Yesterday died last night,
While tomorrow is yet to be born.
But today has captured my love for you
That will carry us into the future and make history.

My Heart II

In the eyes of a man in love,
Rests a woman who is close at heart.
Your kiss I wish for,
Your touch I desire,
Your love is all I need
and will never be forgotten.

My Heart III

The tears have gone away but the pain still lives within.
One day I hope that I can wake up
and just like the tears –
The Pain will be gone too.

Heavenly Flower

Where you belong is where you find yourself... In my heart and with no one else.
The path you chose could never be a mistake; The Love we hold...
A bond that won't break.
The pain you feel, I can feel it too;
I know it's hard to deal but together we can make it through.
If you just stop to look,
The obvious is so clear
Just one more step...
The end is drawing near.
And when you fall weak –
I got your back
And when your eyes leak –
I'll counter attack.
Since you came into my life,
I can see the light,
I can see a brighter day,
I can see you as my wife.
Some things are free –
Others, a hefty price you pay
A sacrifice for love
But it's worth every day.
So glad you came, in the darkness of the hour
You brought light,
     You brought love,
          You brought strength,
               You brought power...
              And I Love you for that...
             My Heavenly Flower.

Winter Love

Snowflakes fall before my eyes as I gaze out of my window pane,
The beautiful sight of winter time, slowly but surely came.
You can hear the brisk wind pounding at the front door
As I embrace the warmth of my cabin,
The fireplace was lit and the time is morning –
The vision is better than you can imagine.
From behind me appears the love of my life,
Her face is lit with a glow,
With hot chocolate in her hand,
Beside me she stands,
As we both enjoy the fall of the snow.
I love her so much –
I can't see us apart and I marvel the day that we met,
As I taste her soft lips and look into her eyes –
Gently my hands caress her neck.
As the day passed and night time fell,
The moon would offer us some light,
Cuddling on the couch –
Holding each other close,
The moment had felt so right.
Wishing it would stay and never go away
I prayed to God above,
Trying my best to hold on to it all –
This precious winter love.

Yesterday's Love

Yesterday's love is gone in the wind,
Wishing it was still there but refusing to pretend.
The beauty of love - no longer exist,
The sweet taste of one's lips so often is missed.
Started out as so right, but ended up so wrong,
Constantly wondering to myself... Where has it all gone?
Many sleepless nights,
Many days gone by,
Many thoughts of you... many tears I cry.
Trying so hard to be strong –
In the mist of the pain,
Through the worst of it all,
Feeling left in the rain.
Somebody please tell me how –
Come show me how to do you start,
How do you pick up the pieces
and mend a lone-broken heart?
Each night I gaze into the sky
And watch the shining stars above,
Can't help but wonder to myself,
What happened to my Yesterday's Love?

It Was Only Yesterday

Yesterday we use to be so close
and today it doesn't even matter,
A bond once so strong,
But today it's torn and shattered.
We don't even know each other – at least not as before
We don't even say I love you - at least not anymore.
A distance has wedged between us
and it seems as if we gave it permission
Your face is no longer clear to me –
No matter how hard I try to envision.
Nonexistent to each other's world,
Sometimes it's hard to believe you're not there
But the coldness of it all –
Sometimes I don't even care.
I leave you to be your way and for me you leave me to be mine,
Somehow, some way, I think of it all and I conclude...
Maybe that's just fine.

Surrendered Heart

It wasn't supposed to happen this way
You invaded my heart without my say.
You came in my life from out of the blue
You opened my eyes to something so new.
You're in comparable to any of my past,
and who would have thought I will fall for you so fast?
My morning flower,
    My breath of air
        My forever precious queen
Be gentle with my heart and please do so by every means.
I tried to deny the way I was feeling,
My mind said no but my heart was so willing.
The seduction of your love came like a thief in the dark
and I was left with no choice,
But to surrender to you my heart.

A Wish and a Promise

Promises are made to be broken
As wishes are made to come true.
But all promises doesn't go broken
And all wishes never follow through.
So I promise to you, to make a wish
To love you until I die,
And I wish that the promise I make to you,
Will never become a lie.

Once in a Lifetime

Many have searched the world
In search for a diamond or two,
and while many continue to search on,
I found my diamond in you.
Indeed you are a treasure to me
 In every tiny bit of the sense,
and I marvel the day I found you,
Despite the circumstance.
Some pass through this lifetime
Never experiencing true love,
A love so unique and sacred ,
A love so rarely heard of.
You have given me so much of you
and I am so glad that you exist,
You are the center of my world
and the source of my happiness.
I am trapped in a realm of love,
Surrounded by a golden gate,
Content with the way I'm feeling –
Convinced this must be fate.
A smile appears on my face,
I'm so grateful that you are mine
A love I will always cherish –
A Love Once in a Life Time.

A Prelude to a Kiss

I see it in your eyes, from far across the room,
You like what you see - and it is me I assume.
I casually break a smile, simply to acknowledge your attention
Nobody else seems to know - or even have suspicion.
The party seems to be nice, but it's not really our cup of tea,
All that seems to really matter, is the energy between you and me.
I compelled myself to approach, neither one of us spoke a word,
With our bodies doing the talking, I'm thinking this is absurd.
Still no one seemed to notice, the interest we had for one another,
No one had a clue, that tonight we would become lovers.
And with my staring into your eyes, I wonder just what all is this,
Not long before I realized- It Was a Prelude to a Kiss!

A Love So Real

I never thought that I would love again,
It happened so fast, it took my head for a spin.
The love you have given me
It feels so good
I'll never let it go,
Even if I could.
I'm yours forever - my heart belongs to you
There's nothing in life - for you I won't do.
You changed my life in such short of a time
You make me so whole and I'm so glad that you're mine.
Your warm soft touch, I really do miss
and with each new day, I yearn for your kiss.
The thought of you alone, brings my body chills
and I marvel that I found - A Love So Real.

Deep Thoughts

I am reaching for a long lost love –
A love that I've been searching for a long time now.
I have let go of the past and I now embrace the present.
This precious love so long overdue is for me as well as for you.
I treasure all the love you have given me,
As well as I have given you...
The love that I have to offer to you is priceless - can't you see?
This love of a lifetime I am yearning to share with you
and it truly, truly had to take a very special love like yours
to pave the way for me to see –
The one who is truly there for me.
The love that you have instilled inside of me, no one can ever take that away.
You have touched my heart and soul very deeply
and you have fulfilled my deepest desires.
I will always and forever be true to your love –
No matter the distance between us.
As the day turns into night,
I find myself retiring early this evening
and as I lay back reminiscing about our sacred moments together,
I'm holding on to the warm, soft and gentle touch of your beauty.
You caring heart and beautiful smile brighten up the darkest of dark nights.
The sweet - sweet touch of your beauty has me so inspired,
I can almost feel your warm touch.
I can't wait to see the sparkles in your eyes again.
The outer glow of your face surrounds the beauty that lies deep inside you.
I cherish every single moment that we have had together.
I was truly blessed to have you as a part of my life
and I hope that you feel the same about me.
Oh, how I could go on and on about so many things,
but I must rest my head now and hopefully dream of you.

Disappearing Diamond

I asked myself ... did I lose a diamond?
I reached in my pocket and it was empty.
I know it was there before!
I backtracked to see if I could find it.
One year later, still no luck - I really must have lost it!

Thinking Back On Us

Thinking back on us is a pleasant thought for me.
How we laughed,
How we cried;
How we made every moment so special.
Nothing can compare to the love we shared.
Every day that goes by makes me want to go back
To when we first fell in love.
Loving you came so natural and for certain, it was true.
I remember all the dinners, movies
and even our most intimate times together.
If I had them to watch on a videotape,
I would watch them over and over.
You give new meaning to the word "Special".
Thinking back on us brings a great joy inside of me.
You were the best woman I ever had and truly the best friend I ever had.
If I could turn back the hands of time,
I would go back to our first days of being together and break the clock,
Hoping time will never advance,
For those were the best days of my life.
My heart beats fast,
My head starts to spin,
I begin to sweat and fall in love with you all over again
When I start, thinking back On Us!

These Three Words

To be there with you right now, will be a dream come true
To have you wrapped in my arms, there is nothing in life I wouldn't do.
I love you so much, in so many ways that words could never express,
Even actions itself would be so hard, but I'll promise to do my best.
To love sometimes is so hard, but with you - you make it so easy
These words I say are sincere and true and I hope and pray that you believe me.
Take my heart into your hands and guard it with your life
For if the Higher Being, God, allows it, then one day you should be my wife.
There's one thing in life I know for sure, that will always and forever be true
And that's the sweet sound of these three words of when I say - I Love You!

Sweet Love

Sweet love, something I never really knew
Lost in a sea of uncertainty, then along came you.
Untamed passion, music to my heart that I've never heard before
A rainbow full of beautiful emotion, I sigh - this experience I adore
A quiet love storm, so gentle with its every breeze
The center of my attraction... satisfaction I can't believe.
A love Goddess, could you actually be so real?
A genuine love, is this actually what I feel?
This parade of marching joy - an unforgettable part of my life
My eyes, they gaze the night time sky - you, my star so bright.
Dazzling...
Your smile, your eyes,
Your being and everything you consist of,
Hungry, I sit, I begin to feast...
Another bite of this sweet love.

From Me to You

I thought that you were gone,
but we found each other again
So glad that I was wrong...
So glad it didn't end.
When I think of you, I think of love
and all that it can be
When I think of love, I think of you,
It come so naturally.
Your beautiful smile,
Your soft creamy skin –
I yearn to touch you right now
Your eyes I adore,
I want you so bad –
I just can't figure out how.
So many miles away we stand,
Precious Love, you are so far...,
Through the midnight sky I search for you –
You are my shining star.
These words they come from out of the blue,
From heart to heart...
From Me to You

Poetic Mind

It was destiny but who knew it before it came about - only God.
What is it that causes our love to soar; higher than a bird,
Stronger than a tornado wind?
It all came about like a summer breeze,
Pleasant as watching the sunrise or the sunset or the beauty in your eyes.
Touched by an angel, trapped in heaven gates –
I've become captured but willing...
Oh, what a wonderful feeling!
Melodies of love echo around
Sounds of my heart beat aloud...
You have me flattered,
I'm tickled like a little child.
Listen to my heart giggle-
Funny, but serious at matter.
Your love I find pure and the taste is so sweet –
I'm hungry and delighted to take one more bite.
and if my appetite is too much,
It's only because I've been starved...
Let me feast...If ever,
It's okay-
I'm crazy in love.
Why is love so crazy?
I can't help but love a love like yours!
Illuminating the dark, you came –
You changed my life...
and for that you will be...
Forever my wife.

Feelings

Rain, lightning, thunder – It's okay...
Smile for me.
Gloomy, cold, frightening - I'll be okay...
I'll smile for you.
You wipe away the moisture from my eyes,
I'm happy for the first time in my life.
I envision your face before my every step,
I'm left with nothing else...
Loving you is my only option.
Tomorrow's sunshine is late
but still there's a summer breeze,
Does it feel good to you?
Cause it feel good to me.
I can wait, but it's not what I want, but it is what I will....
But you already know.
I love you, I need you - I need the love you give
Breathe into my soul...
The reason why I live.

Love and Change

Not quite often do you find someone like you
Who can change a man's life and make it brand-new
Very seldom do you see the man loving the woman
more than the woman loving the man,
Don't ask me why because this is yet for me to understand.
All I know is I love you more than you will ever know
and the full effect of my love I have yet to show.
In time you will see exactly what I mean
If only you can wait you will see what true love brings.
You made me this way, full of love and care
and in return I will always love you and always be there.

Majestic Lady

Out of the corner of my eyes I saw her coming my way,
Her eyes were made of diamonds
Her presence was enveloped by a sweet smell of lovely.
It was she who would be my wife, if only I could get her to look my way.
Building up the courage to speak was not easy, but I finally did.
I cleared my throat, blinked my eyes and she was gone.
Looking frantically all around, I couldn't find her.
Repeating to myself, "I had the chance and blew it! "
I walked away with my head bowed.
Suddenly, a woman's voice whispered in my ear,
"Excuse me sir."
Hoping it was her, I had turned around with a smile of passion
but it was only another woman telling me I had left my umbrella behind.
As the rain began to fall, my mind was left in wonder...
Will I ever get another chance to lay my eyes on that Majestic Lady?

Anniversary

A loving heart like yours is truly hard to find,
Often I don't tell you but I'm so glad that you are mine.
You bring out the best in me in every which way you can,
In my most difficult time of need, right there is where you stand.
The love we share will always be so meaningful and so true,
It's been a year from the sacred day that we both said I do.
I take this day and set it aside and hope to never let go
And for the years to come I want nothing more but to watch our love
steadily grow.
My Love,
        My Queen,
                My Everything,
These words are true I say
I hope just like me, that you do the same and cherish this sacred day.

Precious Queen

Precious queen you are to me
When I think of you, I'm worry free.
You bring great joy into my life
When things were wrong, you made them right.
Your sacred love I do adore
And with each new day, I love you more.
I carry you into my dreams at night
And as if they were you, I hold them tight.
This thing is real between me and you
And never have I felt a love so true.
I promise to protect you from all the rain
From the lonely days and all the pain.
Your love is always safe in my heart
and I pray that this love never falls apart.
You're my flower, my dream, my everything
But most of all, you're my precious queen.

From The Essence of My Soul

The essence of your beauty,
Truly took me by surprise
From the beautiful ways of your personality,
To the beautiful color of your eyes.
I never thought that I would meet someone –
Someone with so much love to share.
Someone who I would be so madly in love with –
Someone so devoted and always there.
From the moment we met in person –
From the moment of our first kiss,
I knew you were my soul-mate to be
and with this I am so convinced.
The distance between us is great
but in time we will soon be together
A commitment we both have made,
For a love that will last forever.
Like precious jewels you are to me
and I'll protect you with my very own life
A sacrifice I'm so willing to make
for the woman that will one day become my wife.
I love you Mamí with all my heart
and it's important that these words be told
A love so great,
So pure, so true...
A love From the Essence of My Soul!

2013 – 2017

~NOW~ Part 2

Reflections

Abandon

Searching for a vein in my arm to deliver a dose of determination,
Fighting against the strong current so as not to become complacent.
Finding myself pacing,
While time is disintegrating;
I'm taking deep breaths while trying to master patience.
I'm wondering what's left?
Or will I even make it...?
Split second decisions,
Do I win or do I lose?
No one knows the outcome
but you still gotta choose.
Standing at the edge... so dangerously close
Emotions mixed –
One day you're cool and the next you're over the cliff.
Gotta watch your every step for all it takes is one slip.
Family don't understand, although they think they do –
I feel it's impossible to, unless it happens to you.
Don't try to walk in my shoes or tell me it'll be okay,
When you haven't been there –only pretending to care
and I know it's not fair because you was there that one time...
Well, that was only one time – out of all this time.
You wasn't there when I was crying,
Moments when I felt like dying;
Moments I fell totally apart...
Moments left in total dark.
With shattered pieces on the floor. ...
Trying to mend a broken heart.
Not a word, not a remark –
Not an utter or a whisper...
Not a father, not a mother, not a brother or a sister...

Black Lives Matter

I can't breathe!
I feel like I'm being choked out,
Life is flashing before me,
Yet they ignore me,
Only to squeeze tighter,
My head is feeling lighter.

Don't just stand there
and watch somebody tell them to stop.
Stop Police Brutality & wrongful convictions
Stop pretending we're not witnessing modern day lynching;
Finally, it seems the world is paying attention.
I'm watching the news but they keep failing to mention
What about all these wrongful conviction.

I hope you are listening,
I'm no longer whispering,
I'm screaming at the top of my lungs,
Hoping & pleading for somebody to come.
Please don't just do nothing!
Everybody can do something.
You can retweet, repost,
Don't tell the least instead tell the most,
Until they are chanting "Free Ricky Kidd!" from coast 2 coast,
Until I'm finally free and we can finally toast.
A Victory won by the voice of the people;
Black lives do matter
and we all should be treated equal.

Resiliency

Resiliency – That's me.
Lungs filled with Smoke & Fumes,
Still I crawled from beneath the rubble,
Sure, I've struggled in the midst of debris,
Sure, I was supposed to drown while being lost at sea.
You can call me Ricky or Resiliency.
Turbid winds below,
Face buried beneath the snow,
My entire life was frost bit,
When my existence went numb,
My Spirit refuse to quit.
Few could ever handle their life being dismantled,
Surrounded by total darkness,
Not so much as even a candle.
I was forced to become the light,
Illuminating everything in sight;
I was forced to become the oxygen
If ever I was to breathe again.
Floundering on my pathway
I was almost half way
Only to realize I was going the wrong way.
What I discovered more stunning
was that the Calvary wasn't coming.
I was trapped inside a dungeon
but never feeling like I was done in.
Maybe it was because I'd let the Son in?
Try living in a place without the sun in?
Try being buried alive and still managing to survive?
Try walking among the dead but refusing to die;
Refusing to capitulate,
Appealing to a higher fate,
Knowing in my growing many blessings await
The more I orchestrate
comes the revealing of my brilliance.
How I made it is the question,
but there's no question to my resilience.

Take to the Sky

They tried to kill my destiny,
They tried to kill the best of me,
When they arrested me for a murder in the 1st degree...
Falsely,
Must I not fail to mention,
Life without parole was my sentence,
I was defenseless...
My lawyer was incompetent
While the prosecutor was relentless.
Pretending to truly care about Justice
When it was just about winning.
My nightmare was just beginning...
I was pinned in and I couldn't get out,
Mouth wide open but nothing seemed to come out,
So much could prove my innocence but it didn't come out-
They sold me out like slaves being sold in the south.
On my trip to the plantation
I was thinking whatever happened to reasonable doubt?
Pondering to myself, they trying to alter my route.
They trying to offset my sprout... afraid of how I'll turn out.
Attempting to make me out of a black slave
Only made me black & brave;
They expected me to cave or go crawl in a grave,
Yet I rise unscathed...
Looking forward to better days.
Yeah, I know they are amazed,
Yeah, I was hit but only grazed,
I was under their attack
 but overcame... unfazed.
They overestimated themselves
While underestimating my depth,
Now I'm over determined to do something good with myself,
I'm feeling good about myself
and I'm ready to Fly-
Wings spread like an eagle,
It's Time to Take to The Sky!

A Country Lost & Gone Astray

Looking at the world from my Prison Cell Window Pane,
The world is feeling pain,
Many things have changed.
Tragedy is dominating our news,
While violence has made its way to our schools.
Politicians making promises
but they're nothing more than a ruse.
Feeling unamused,
Feeling unenthused,
Feeling like a refugee,
Who feels like waking in my shoes?
Our Justice system is a subterfuge.
Subterranean deals keep us subject to mass incarceration,
Black annihilation,
False prosecutions without reparations.
We rather face amusement than to face our nation,
With these mass shootings, it got me contemplating.
We should be conversating yet we're congregating,
We should be taking action,
Yet we steady laughing... Now Breathe.
They say everything isn't as simple as black & white,
but that all depend on whether you're black or white.
They shouldn't have killed Michael Brown
Rather wrong or right?
 Nor Eric Gardner or Tamir Rice.
Police Brutality is Finally Coming to light...
That's why we're coming to fight.
We got to stay in the fight!
No more being polite.
We gotta demand some change,
We gotta solidify our demands and stop settling for change.
Too many guns on our streets,
Too many suicide teens,
Too many times have we seen too many broken up dreams.

Our babies are dying,
While our soldiers are dying...brave.
We know they're brave;
Putting it all on the line...
Billions being spent on a war that's not ours,
They coming home with scars then we leave them to starve.
Homes they barely got,
Some even sleeping in cars.
Have we come a long way?
Or have we gone too far?
Terrorism abroad is now in our backyard
Too is much on our plate-
While we're Losing sight of what's at stake,
We must go on high alert,
Before we discover it's too late.
Destruction is standing at the gate
and if we wait we won't escape.
We just watching as we're toppling —
A country lost & gone astray!

Words from the Wrongful Convicted

Here's the situation,
A wrongful incarceration
A 19-year rotation
Imagine what I've been facing.
Every day as I'm awakened
The pain is unimaginable,
Anxiety unmanageable,
A freedom so deserved
Yet a freedom unattainable.
Tell me, where did lady justice go?
Or has she fell asleep while walking her beat?
Justice gone wrong... is it only for the elite?
Looks like she done took a peek.
It's supposed to be neutral
Where she honors the facts,
But she ain't honoring Jack!
Is it because I am black?
Or has she been manipulated
by the politics of winning?
Back door deals-
Why they skinning and grinning?
Say they care about the truth
but they are only pretending.
Look at the money they're spending
While the innocent spending life without parole
or some different type of sentence.
You hit them with the truth
but they're so damn relentless,
They offer no apology for being so pretentious;
A crime in broad daylight,
The unsuspected suspects
The one you tend to trust in,
The ones you go to elect.
You promise to tell the truth
While they promise to protect a lie!

I promise this is the truth,
My innocence is not a lie,
Now that you know the truth join the movement
and don't just standby.
My facts, they stand out...
My plea, please stand up!
For injustice, let's turn up...
Till I'm free, don't give up!
Many faces in these places are facing a grim reality
of a broken system,
Screaming out loud,
Hoping somebody will listen.
We care about so much but not much for those in prison
Even when we see the statistics of innocence has risen.
It's time we rise too!
Justice need you!

As A Matter of Fact

Sometimes word aren't enough,
Dreams deferred,
Bearing burdens in the rough,
Vision blurred.
By a merciless system unjust,
Who cared when none dare call it a conspiracy?
Masterminds in the trenches,
Plotting routinely to erase the surrounding fences.
Through eyes like mine
Carrying the torch of legacy,
Oblivious to reality, others clearly don't see.
There's no escape,
No safe place,
Insidious the tragic fate,
I'm left to contemplate.
Among the Perils of Prisoners
Seeking redemption through my deliverance,
While they fail to do me justice.
Innocent I am,
While innocent bystanders watch them handcuff us.
Yearning to be free,
To breathe and chase your dreams,
Fulfill your beautiful potential as a dignified human being.
What is democracy when the innocent suffer
in the clutches of wicked hypocrisy?
Clutching my belly from the wounds of a knife in me.
Barley am I breathing,
Scarcely aware while vaguely somebody's screaming,
"We gotta stop the bleeding!"
What's Freedom of anything?
When your voice can be silenced, by the sound of a gavel
Our courtrooms have become violent!
We must Demand Change!
We must bring our P.O.W.S (Prisoners of Wrongful Conviction) home.
Uhuru Sasa! (Freedom Now!)

Yes, I will Arrive

I wanna smile and find reason to celebrate this pious day,
A moment in the present,
Yet remembering the journey of days and years –
Some with oversized Joy,
Others with oversized tears.
Some filled with courage,
Others filled with fears...
An unspeakable experience and reflective story of triumph.

Who can dare stand and say I have been beaten,
Yet I haven't been beating?
I have been betrayed,
Yet I've never strayed.
Daily executions of excavating to the soul's core essence,
Discovery of a real man,
Scattered bones of an adolescent.
Managing to topple obstacles on my path to progression,
Taking a moment of silence,
Thankful for every lesson...
Counting every blessing.
Casualties all around me,
While I'm committed to keeping it stepping.
Miracles in the making-
Some very clear,
Some in disguise.
Knowing in due time,
I most certainly will arrive.
Yes... I will arrive!

Move Along People, There's Nothing Here Left to See

Move along people, there's nothing here left to see.
It's just me, struggling to see the forest from the trees,
Trying my best to be more than the eye can see.
The rain drops falling is really my tears,
The bravado I'm displaying masquerades my fears –
Nineteen long years, fast approaching twenty,
There shouldn't have been any,
Feeling damn near on empty.
I suppose my innocence isn't relevant?
Or that injustice really isn't prevalent...
Or that Lady Justice isn't so benevolent?
Or that I'm not really living in these elements?
My mind grows fatigued,
Fighting a liberty that's under siege...
Move along people, there's nothing here left to see.

Other than me, grasping for air and reaching for life-
Gotta resuscitate myself or risk losing my life.
Was it a gun or a knife?
What has pierced my flesh?
 All I know is that I'm bleeding,
Dancing close with death.
Have they made an arrest?
Have the tracked down the looter?
Did they get a description?
Do they know it's the prosecutor?
Do they know that she don't like losing...
Purposely making my facts confusing?
Will you tell them that the power they gave her
Was the same power she was abusing?
She had an accomplice, so I was told;
Old white man wearing a black robe.
They escaped in a black Porsche...
I hear their hideout is in the Circuit Court.
Don't just stand there focused on me...
Move along people, there's nothing here left to see.

Unless you gone be a witness?
Unless you gone help prove who did this?
I'm feeling kinda faint,
Somebody check my wrist...
Somebody tie off the wound,
I can't breathe...
Make me some room.
I'm trapped inside of a room.
My legal team is my only hope,
Because of them I'm not broken,
I found my voice so these words could be spoken.
My strength was depleted
but I'm back on my feet
Got some places to go & some people to meet.
Move along people, there's nothing here left to see.

The Sixth Dimension

Tormented by the anguish of a false imprisonment wasn't enough,
I was struck!
By a blunt sharp instrument from behind...
When I came to I was blind,
Paralyzed in my spine.
Unable to reach, screech or scream.
All I could make out was the light beaming overhead
as if a surgery was taken place...
I sensed a strong impression I had been misplaced,
Or an attempt to be erased.
Voices around me competed for my attention,
I was in the Sixth Dimension...
Or was I just in prison?
A non-functioning distress button caused me more distress-
A false imprisonment while already in prison is what I began to see.
When the lights finally dimmed,
There was the shadow of concrete
and steel located in all four corners of the room;
Or was it really a room?
More like a cave in the middle of the artic
It was like arsenic.
Slowly you die while still trying to live,
and if the desire isn't strong
Then surely the heart will give.
The clanging of keys constantly disrupting your dreams
and even in reality nothing is as though it seems.
Is this the price of sin or what evil men bring?
No matter how hard you sleep it's not a portal to escape...
For the only way out is to fully awake.

A Fools Benediction

A hero
He once ran into a burning building to save his Glock 40,
Climbing the steps of 10 stories.
Once making it out alive he was praised with glory.
He once gave food to his neighbor with five kids
Apparently forgetting what he just did
It was less than a week ago that he stood on the front deck
Serving Miss Annette.
Handing over his crack cocaine
As she handed over her welfare check
and the last we checked,
He was a gentleman & a scholar
The streets knew his name,
He endured fame chasing the mighty dollar
He would take little boys who didn't have much to eat,
Give 'em a dope pack trying to put them on their feet.
He ran from the strong,
but preyed on the weak.
He once did a good deed
Covered a dead body with a sheet.
Little girls he enticed with his glittery chains.
Within a blink of an eye, their innocence would die!
Coulda' been a butter fly but he chose to be a moth
 and for the decisions he made,
This is how we send him off.
So long you damn fool, because we sure don't want you back!
You lived your life out of spite,
Leaving a negative impact.
You coulda" did more-
Making a positive difference but you didn't,
We glad you're gone...
This is a Fools Benediction.

Encouraging Words

The day I was arrested, it came to me unexpected
It came when I was infected,
Lack of information left me unprotected.
But now I seek to correct it-
The value of freedom I've grown to respect it.
I found myself mentally dead, but now I'm resurrected.
The truth I no longer reject it,
Taking charge of my own life, I found was the best bet.
Best bet I'm living right now,
I put down the nonsense
and picked up the King's Crown,
I'm King now,
My thoughts went from dull to keen now,
I Dream now and the prospects of my future...
They gleam now!
You ask how?
Well, it was information that was brought my way,
It was brothers like them who've done paved the way
It was Gangs, Guns and Drugs that I gave away
and now today, I can proudly say that for me & you both
There's a better way...
For me and you both they got a word to say;
Rather, a story to share.
I think you'll find that they really do care
and I respectfully ask that you open your ears
But not just to hear,
But to also receive
Try to find it in your mind to embrace & believe,
and know that in your heart...
You too can achieve.

Emotions

Managing these emotions is like riding a rollercoaster
and though I'm getting closer, I'm not feeling like I'm supposed to.
What do you suppose I do?
After all of the appeals that I've been through...
After all of the hills I've traveled through?
Feeling unsure, although the facts are pretty sure.
How much longer must I endure?
Traveling through these winding roads,
Hoping that one of these mines don't explode!
Trying to stop my mind from going rogue...
Physical changes of my body getting old.
The sun is shining but their hearts are still cold.
I've proven my innocence, but they still won't let me go!
 When will they let me go?
When will they embrace the truth?
When will we say "Enough" and hold them accountable?
They're acting like animals...
They're acting like cannibals...
They're hungry for innocent flesh;
Devouring till nothing is left.
I'm standing despite being left!
They're dodging me,
First right and then left –
No apology, remorse or regret.
I'll be fighting till there's nothing left...
I'll be fighting until my very last breath!
I'll be fighting until they give me justice or death!

1974

I'm thankful to God for the creative imagination,
Bringing forth the force of inspiration – that's me.
Meditating in solitude,
Refusing to capitulate
Through these windings roads my story grows.
Maximizing my deliberate intentions is the only mission.
I'm thankful to my mother for creating this beautiful black brother
and thoughtful of my father,
Knowing he had to be a thinker yet a slick talker.
Finding ways to embody knowledge and wisdom,
Over-standing the black man's current condition,
Half the man they are,
With half of a vision.
So I reflect on my own growth & charm,
How did I do it?
Long enduring through massive storms...
A King was born.
Who could tell when she held me in her arms?
Through knowledge I am armed and it's time to move on.
Get ready everybody...
I'm on my way home.

Seeing the Forest from the Weeds

I know it may be hard to see that God is real,
When what was once safe has become "Killing Fields".
It feels surreal...
It seems at odds,
I keep asking myself, "Where is our God? Our Father, which art in heaven" Thy kingdom come
The world is done
 Look at what we've done?
We've mistreated one another with malice and aggression,
With so much hatred and rage
Holy wars have been waged!
Blacks against whites,
Blue against red
Everybody is talking,
Ignoring what's being said.
Pretending to be so different
Pretending to be prestigious
I turn on the news and it's hard to even believe this!
Where are you God, when your presence is so needed?
We all want to win but we're all being defeated.
Car bombs blowing up
Crazed men shooting,
Black lives dying...
Police lives ruined.
Racism gone wild
What the hell are we doing?
My heart goes out to the LGBT
To Philando Castille, may you rest in peace
As we try to find peace... the whole world is in grief.
You died too soon, just for being who are
The night is dark and we've lost too many stars –
They say "We've come a long way",
I say we've gone too far.

I cried half the day, I'll cry the rest tomorrow
Feeling distraught and disturbed
Feeling bewildered and baffled
As the daily news unfolds, I'm watching our country unravel
Humanity is being dismantled
We're taking aim at our own destruction
We're sowing the wrong seeds, while reaping the repercussions.
 I'm hearing the discussions and I'm feeling so disgusted!
Our politicians can't be trusted,
So who are we supposed to trust in?
United we once stood, now defiantly we divide...
Our nation's unrest will result in our nation's suicide.

Look No Further Than Yourself

Your Chanel' Shades got you catching shade,
Got you looking like you're paid –
You just got paid, but it's already gone,
Just copped the new iPhone.
You got the latest everything, so they think you're everything,
Got your hair done, nails done
and your whip is clean.
Tank on full, while bank on empty.
Body on bang, but what about your brain?
What about your kids and their college tuition?
You think you're on point, but really you're missing it.
You talk a big game but you hardly ever listen.
You love the attention,
But you don't pay attention.
Your past bills stamped delinquent-
Had the money in your hand, but still you spent it.
Said you bought your own home,
But really it's rented.
In the public your shine is on,
Back at home your lights are off
They try to tell you but your head is hard,
That only means your ass is soft.
You wanna be a boss,
While failing to weigh the cost-
So every time you gain, you're really taking a lost.
Looking for fortune & fame but never looking to find yourself.
So when it all doesn't change
and you're looking to place blame...
Look no further than yourself

Good Cop, Bad Cop

Good Cop awakes each day with a genuine motivation...
Bad Cop is quick to shoot without hesitation.

Good Cop helps an old lady get across the street...
Bad Cop sees a criminal in every black man he meets.

Good Cop goes into a hostile situation at the risk of his life...
Bad Cop ain't bout to chance it,
So he shoots without thinking twice.

Good Cop, there are millions,
They make up a vast portion protecting our nation...
Bad Cop, they slip through the cracks,
Don't really care about blacks and mess up the equation.

Good Cop, supposed to protect & serve our community,
Not protect & serve their unity...
Bad Cop, training day was only a movie –
No one meant for you to act that way for real.

Good Cop investigates a case and follows the clues...
Bad Cop can care less about guilt or innocence
and make up their own rules.

Better Days

When the chips are down and your smile is really a frown
and you're crying to yourself when no one else is around...
Praying 4 Better Days.

Hoping for the best not quite sure if this is already it,
Thinking about all that's lost, so much you start feeling sick...
Praying 4 Better Days.

Tear ducks dry, you done cried your last tear.
But the pain never goes,
Emotions paralyzed & froze...
Praying 4 Better Days.

Sunshine days, blue skies, blue rays-
You can see it but you can't feel it,
You can smell it, but you can't taste it...
Praying 4 Better Days.

Nineteen years, still caught up in the fight-
While the powers to be still won't make it right.
Your reason for holding on,
 is one day they might...

Pray With Me For Better Days!

Cynthia

Is it something I said? Is it something that I've done?
Because your silence is deafening,
It has me spun.
I take pen & paper to express my thoughts,
Share my ideas and convey my fears...
Still in all, it seems to fall on deaf ears.
Questions & concerns pertaining to my case,
As they reach your desk they seem to be erased...
As if I'm out of place.
To even suggest or speak on what should be done,
I've written 4 times but you have failed to respond.
I'm grateful in heart but troubled in the spirit...
My communications matter but it's as if you don't want to hear it.
I love what you do but I just want to be acknowledged.
Just wanna be heard...
I know you are busy but that much I deserve.
The suspects escape Justice and the State seem to follow suit,
They won't do the right thing...
Unless we compel them to.
Close off all exits;
Anticipate their aversion,
The truth they can't handle... so they will create a diversion.
And if we're not smart and take the preemptive measures,
They will surely take theirs in an attempt to be clever.
Losing is hard-
Don't know how much more I can weather,
Justice is elusive,
This time we gotta get her....
The brief was well put but it doesn't create pressure!
The state needs pressure!
What are we doing to create that matter?
Absent its presence,
It won't really matter.

Sure we should win,
We should have already won -3 courts ago but it didn't get done.
Can't take for granted,
This current proceeding...
Then look at my kids knowing it's a dad they're needing.
I appreciate your help,
It all seem to be fate,
But justice must be delivered... it can no longer wait.
I know I am the client and in a way, you are the boss,
So after receiving this letter, I hope we can talk.
Take care be blessed.

Modern Day Lynching

I was sitting at the table watching it all unfold,
It went down so cold, this is how the story goes…
To my right was the jury, seated in two rows.
To my left, a set of prosecutors,
Locked and ready to go.
To my front was a grand wizard,
Who was wearing a black robe…
Now how was I supposed to know that the prosecutor was actually his lover?
That my trial was really just a cover…
and that this was a modern-day lynching?
I was sitting there defenseless,
While my defense lawyer was only pretending.
Their guns started shooting live rounds while mine were shooting blanks!
I tried to hide under the table but I was being flanked…
No chance of survival –
No chance I would make it…
No chance of a deal and if they had offered,
I wouldn't take it!
I was going down in a room full of eyes,
While they stood over me screaming, "Die nigga, die!"
Kneeling down in a crouched position,
I screamed back, "Why, tell me why?"
While my lawyer stood acting shocked and surprised.
I was lying in a pool of blood when the judge said, "All rise!
Get his ass out of here!
Give his ass 100 years and never mind the critical facts
His only crime is being black!
Never mind his cries of being falsely accused
We'll bury his ass behind our complicated rules!"
The audience seemed amused…
Maybe they felt like justice was done.
Maybe they didn't care because it wasn't their son,
Or their brother, or their father.
So they didn't even bother!
And so the story goes –
I was headed upstate.

The ambush was over and I was sealed to my fate.
But wait...
They underestimated my depth and miscalculated my faith...
They forgot that God is great!
You oughta seen the look on their faces when I showed back up,
Gave back two life sentences and told 'em, "Here, take that!"
Put their face to my back and told them I'll be back.
Quietly, they sat because they knew that I meant that.
I redeveloped my facts, became determined to win.
So I got my second wind, with people who knew how to win.
The state's case was weakening
Their faces were sunken in
Those who walked out of my life, started peaking in.
Yeah, I started to smile... yeah, I started to grin.
Yeah, it was looking grim till I started seeking "Him".
Once He came in, He repurposed my life.
He took back everything wrong and made everything right
Turned my pain into purpose
Told me to follow my passion and I would find my purpose.
Told me to let go of revenge because it was fleeing and worthless,
Said He would take what they did and make it all worth it.
So now I see that I am worthy
So I'm sho' bout to work it!
Justice gone wrong...
But it ended so perfect.

Unwanted Vacation

Dreaming in 3D...
Traveling in a dimension beyond what the eyes can see.
I was trying to do me when it caught up with me;
A 20yr getaway on an island with no shoreline.
They said I was guilty of a crime,
So they left me behind.
Checked me into a room, said it was the best that they got;
My amenities was a desk, a steel toilet and a cot.
I asked the doorman if he would be coming back,
He responded, "Maybe, maybe not."
I said, "If this is a joke then you can go ahead and stop"
and without looking back, he said, "It's not!"
The doormen were many, the guests like me, even greater –
Found myself in the cafeteria, waiting on a waiter.
While everyone only had 5 minutes to eat,
Then back to your feet...
Failure to comply and they'll modify your suite.
Waited in line to access the phone,
I tried to call but no one was home...
Look like I was all alone.
Tried calling the travel agency that was responsible for this trip,
All she could say was, "I'm sorry, I trip."
Quivering at the lip, I was a tear away from a cry,
A heartbeat away from a die.
If only I could die. Except my heart wouldn't give,
So I decided to live.
I made it my business to get down to business,
I returned to my religion and started having visions.
Started getting visits, started making gains...
Started making connections that bring about a change.
I took one blink of an eye and it was just Him and I.
He told me I had a purpose and to follow my mission.
He told me that He loved me and that He'd guide me out of prison...
All I needed to do was listen.
True to his promise I got a new flight ticket...
Now I'm standing at the gate, all they got to do is click it.

Stand

Trying to see it from their point of view,
Why is it different from what everyone else view?
Why is it so hard to do what they're supposed to do?
When the truth is so pure-
It's not even obscure?
It's not up for debate, but they say I filed it too late
But wait, when is the truth ever too late?
To leave the innocent in prison, you want us to believe it's ok
No! It's never ok, despite what they say;
The truth is the truth
    and it should always have its place.
It should never be erased...
It should never be replaced with technicalities of law –
I'm thinking, "What a disgrace!"
Is this the new norm we face?
Where the truth no longer matters
    and where justice is overlooked over a technical matter?
Our history's dark chapters are being written again
    But we don't have to let it stand,
Nor should we pretend.
All we have to do...
    is **STAND**!

Innocent Prayer

Camera lens out of focus,
Picture me trying to stay focused
A lot of anxiety but limited motion
Another year is fast approaching –
Counting on a system that's obviously broken...
Waiting to prove the truth that has already spoken.
What am I to do?
I suppose we ought to pray,
I suppose we ought to say,
"Our Father, which art in heaven,
Send us your blessings.
Make them correct this,
Make them respect this...
No longer reject this,
Please hear our message...
We're in need of intercession.

Day Dreaming

Eyes closed, mind open
Visions of a free man...
Long walks going nowhere,
While the kids in the park playing;
Picnic basket, blades of grass,
Plenty of trees as far as you can see.
Some take it for granted...
But not me.
Twenty years wishing that you had it – that's me.
I want to water a plant and cook on a stove,
Drive a new car that I never drove;
Turn in state uniforms and wear "real" clothes
  and take the time to smell a rose...
I wanna eat with a fork,
Stay out till after dark;
Sit on a front porch
  and hear the dogs bark....
I wanna laugh till I cry,
Without having to be afraid to cry.
I wanna say "Good Morning" to my kids
  and never have to say goodbye.
As I write, I cry
Easy to assume as to why –
They keep standing in my way,
While I'm just trying to get by.

Innocent Lives Matter

Embracing the possibilities of endless possibilities.
Assessing the probability of what they'll probably do with me.
Will they set me free or let injustice be?
I'm leaning on the door hoping for victory.
I'm yearning to explore what life has in store for me.
I'm visualizing all the many things I can be.
Wanting my life to matter in the present and the latter-
Astounding growth and development
But without my freedom what will it matter?
Will they ever recognize the truth or will it even matter?
Innocent lives matter!

Right Crime, Wrong Man

Accused of a crime that I didn't commit
While they knew all along who actually did it.
Waiting to be acquitted,
While the real person acknowledged that they did it!
If it were you, wouldn't you be livid?
What would you do if you really had to live it?
Give me a break!
I'm doing my best not to break...
I'm fighting so hard,
I just need a break.
I just need your support so that my spirit don't break.

Seize the Moment

Waiting to seize the moment so I can own it
Never would have reaped it,
If I never would have sown it -
Discovered my true path and now I'm on it.
Granny always told me:
"Success is for those who really want it and for those who persevere."
I think I've shown it!
Externally, I'm waiting on my freedom,
Internally, I already own it.
If only I would have known it back then what I know now.
Back then I wore a gold chain, right now I wear a king's crown...
I'm a king now!
I dream now,
Realizing everything wasn't what it seemed...
Wow!
Poor choices I was making,
But a better man is in the making.
Thanking God that I made it,
While still hoping that I make it.

Cherish the Day

People hurting,
Undeserving,
Families burdened...
Highway shootings got us in our cars swerving.
Feeling nervous about our future.
Seems like we only have more violence to look forward to-
Blood stains on the Bible in the midst of revival...
Suddenly you're forced to consider your survival.
Pain in my Heart,
Tears in my eyes;
Knees on the floor...
While asking God why?
How did we get to this place?
Where nothing is of value, including human life?
Officer screaming, shots fired and end up losing his life.
Now what about his wife... what about his kids?
Crying throughout the night,
Wondering what type of life will they live?
We trying to give everything we got while wondering,
When will it give?
Little babies closing their eyes
While parents expecting them to awake...
Never imagining in their minds,
A precious life they would take.
Lives are being lost while congress gets lost in debates.
This is the world we face as real tears pour down my face.
These images are painted in blood...
They're impossible to erase!
We got our priorities misplaced,
We've taken our eyes off the road-
Moving fast, we're about to crash...
The casualties untold.
Young looters turn into shooters caring less about death,
The whole nation can't breathe...
We're being strangled to death-
We're trying to figure out what's next.

Mangled dreams and shattered hope,
You tilt the bottle;
He takes a smoke...
Futile attempts to try and cope-
I'm trying to stay focused without a scope.
My mind is strong but my heart is broke!
The beautiful sky keeps losing its stars,
These uncertain times is leaving us scarred!
I cried my last tear,
No more left for tomorrow-
Unsure of the future but won't let it get in my way...
Learning to embrace what I love
and to Cherish the Day.

Christ, The Game Changer

Young brotha running the streets
Thinking he was playing Monopoly with his life,
But it was more like Scrabble...
Only he couldn't find the words to save his life.
So the game became Sorry.
He knew he was a pawn in the game of Chess,
Trying to make it to the other side before meeting Death...
But the deck was stacked –
Simply because he was black!
Still, it didn't stop his dreams of growing from a pawn to a bishop,
To a rook or a queen.
Tried his hands at Spades,
But he kept getting set;
So he tried rolling the dice but never had enough to cover the bet.
Moved on to playing Trouble –
Kept him in a lot of trouble...
He sat down to play Dominoes but he had too many doubles.
He tried his hand at basketball but never could get his shot to fall.
Russian Roulette was out of his league,
21 Black Jack was more his speed.
Finally he was winning... but was overcome by greed.
His life was a Twister-
He never could Connect Four;
Even a friendly game of Darts,
He could never get on it the board.
His family was at Feud and his life was in Jeopardy.
The Price Was Never Right while he continued spinning his wheels
For a fortune...
His ambitions were vast
Yet, he could never succeed at Uno.
He thought, if only he could play Golf-
Maybe he could hit a hole in one;
Searching all over the world...
But never seeking The Son!
Always seeking to win,
Not knowing he had already won-
His victory in life was never hidden in a game...
It was The Blood on the Cross that made everything change.

Family Matters
Part 2

A Strong Black Woman

Gravity is not enough to keep you down,
Neither the weight of the world on your shoulders,
Now much older. ...
I can see how you made it through the rape of a slave master,
Those lousy bastards!
I can picture your eyes closed hoping it goes faster.
No wave can batter you,
Spousal abuse didn't shatter you,
Deprivation & degradation of your community;
You were shatter proof.
The mystery to your history in why you never broke,
Technology can finally tell the story.
It was your DNA...
and it continues to be.
Why do you continue to be so strong, even as you continue to be so wronged?
Is it because you are Black?
Bold in your presence & beauty,
The world has no choice but to take notice of your Nudity.
You are a part of a man, yet stand on your own,
Taking from his rib to become his backbone.
You're the last one standing, when everyone else is gone.
You're the baddest creation one could ever assume,
For even those that study you must derive from your womb.
Stack the deck against you and you still had a full house –
The deck was stacked against you when you had a full house.
Your belly would be on empty when you finally got to sleep;
Finally made it home from work,
The kids finally got to eat.
They got your sons in the streets,
The ramifications of a deadbeat, Dad.
Forced to be the mother, father and grandmother
To a teen with low self-esteem,
Giving it up, trapped in a daydream.

Young kids murdered in the streets
All you hear is their screams,
Your other son hauled off to prison,
It all seems so extreme.
Pick up your grandbaby while you pick up your son's call –
Try picking up the pieces, when they all so small.
There's nothing like the beauty of a woman standing tall,
Battering rams can't knock you down –
You done been through it all.
I wonder if they would believe me if I told them what I saw?
Encircled by lions yet you defeated them all.
I am in awe and you are so stunning –
The essence of who you are...
A Strong Black Woman.

Dear Momma I'm All Done Playing

Dear Momma,

I already made you hurt when I come pushing out at birth. Bet you wasn't thinking about that, when dad was trying to get under your skirt? Raised in a world against us, but somehow you made it work. I remember how hard you worked, so I went out and got me some "work". Police used to raid the spot but I had it hidden in the dirt. They tried to take me then... but all they got was a smirk. You taught me right from wrong but I wanted to learn on my own. I was tired of being a kid, I guess I wanted to be grown. Racing in the streets of life, running every red light; thought I was so damn bright, Man, you were so damn right. Trying to be a Superman, Batman, Spiderman... thought I was a superhero, flying on that super "indo". Thinking back in retrospect, it was kinda foolish though. You gave me life and I was your world. I shot the dice, now look at my world. Look at me now, see past the smile; only you can see the pain, you know your child. Living in regret, it's hard not to do. Can't get past the mistakes and the pain I caused you. I don't know what I would do if I ever lost you. This is something I wouldn't want to face... you could never be replaced. Filled with a lot of love, but also with a little disgrace, I know I let you down when I landed in this place. But I'm in a new space and I got a new stance. I became a new man; finally got what you were saying.... Recess is over and "I'm All Done Playing".

In Case I Didn't Make It

A precious life in our hand,
Yet for granted, we take it.
Tell 'em all that I tried,
Just in case I didn't make it.
Wrong turns, bad directions,
On a path of imperfections...
But I found it, became the light,
No one ever could mistake it.
I broke a few hearts as well as some promises
But I promise, it was never my intention to break it.
Tell 'em all that I'm sorry, just in case I didn't make it.
Created some laughs,
Didn't we all laugh?
Boy did we laugh-
But it was never meant to last.
Forever so thankful for God crossing our paths.
Lofty dreams of changing the world,
Seeing the world, it changed me.
In pursuit of finding meaning,
Low & behold I found me!
Kept it real, at least I tried,
Saw no need in trying to fake it...
Tell 'em how I was, just in case I didn't make it.
Loved my family,
Loved my friend;
They were with me till the end.
Some did better than others but at least they didn't pretend.
Tell 'em how much I love them...
Just in case I didn't make it,
Tell 'em that I fought but my body couldn't take it –
Five more miles to heaven,
I think I'm gonna make it.
The guy lying there as you all cry & stare,
Could you tell him that I love him and that I wanted to be there?
Could you tell him I enjoyed the ride and it was a ride worth taking?
Could you tell him, will you tell?
Just in case I didn't make it.

Dear You

The echoes of silence has begun to suffocate my ability to breathe and the vivid picture of life seems to fade. Finally, today I woke up from my sleep to realize I have been dreaming all along. The piercing pain alarmed me that it is definitely reality. In a desert land an old man circles me repeating, "The cavalry isn't coming." I wish he would stop, but he won't and I see why. The cavalry really isn't coming.

For almost 17 years now. I have been abducted and tucked away in a dark location. Yet I've managed to call out for help. I've managed to obtain pens & paper to write out my pleas and the cold breeze of my wrongful conviction has blown them right to your mailbox. But it is as if the house has been abandoned. Tears wash my face as I organize these expressions because I have come to my wits end. I simply do not know what to say or write, or articulate to garner any serious interest in my situation from close family & friends. Or should I correctly recite the previous sentence as long distant family & friends or non-existent family and friends. When I awake I wonder why do I dream of people coming to help rescue me, restore me...Yet when I am asleep I dream of all those who love me, yet ignore me. Silence has never been so loud! Where you wish everyday it would go away and be replaced with waves of noise, sounds of your name being called for mail or a visit... A Christmas card or an "I haven't forgotten you" card, a "Stop wishing I was active in your life" card. Maybe I would have stopped then, instead of only realizing it now.

How many times do you try to speak to someone then they refuse to speak back? How many times do you invite someone over without having them ever come over? How many times will a girl call a guy without him ever calling back? How many letters will a man send to family & friends without them ever responding back? As if he never wrote in the first place?

You will more likely hear the cry of a baby locked in a car and come to his aid before you will ever acknowledge mine. You will likely rescue a dog or cat before you make any real efforts to try and rescue me. You will likely donate to a worthy cause elsewhere before it even crosses your mind that charity starts at home. You will likely wear a "Justice for Trayvon Martin" shirt before you ever consider wearing a "Justice for Ricky Kidd" shirt. You will likely talk to everyone you come in contact with about the tragedy of the 20 children slain, before you talk to one person about the tragedy of my case situation.

If you broke your leg and had it in a cast, you would likely ask more people to sign your cast than you would ask them to sign my petition.

Somehow, people who I imagined cared have not cared enough. When I imagined my case to be relevant, it has not been relevant enough. When I hoped to be an important person in your life, I have not been important enough. As I developed, changed and became a better person, it wasn't enough to warrant your attention.

Increasingly. I feel as if my existence doesn't matter, as if my wrongful conviction doesn't matter, as if even my few accomplishments do not matter. One of the worst feelings to wake up to is the feeling that you don't matter in a place, in a world, in an individual's life... But somewhere someplace and to some people, I do matter and one day I will matter to millions. Using my life to make a difference in theirs. I'm sorry I didn't make much of a difference in yours and I only wish you would have made a difference in mine.

I'm moving on now - I have a long road until the next town. No need to keep sitting here, the old man was right and you have convinced me... "The cavalry really isn't coming. "
Just want you to know that today, I have come to terms with that.

If It Wasn't For a Mother

Out of the birth canal
Comes a baby's cry but a mother's smile.
Every woman on earth,
Those who have given birth,
Knows of this wonderful feeling.
 Cradled in a mother's arms,
She looks down upon her child,
Ready to answer to the call of duty;
        To nurture,
                To provide and support.
She is ready to go wherever motherhood takes her.
As her child begins to grow,
She never knows what road or path they will go.
Be it may the world stage or an early grave,
Her child may become an athlete,
    A doctor,
        A scholar,
                A banker or a bank robber.

Early in the beginning,
Looking through her prism,
Whatever she had envisioned...
Surely it was never prison.
Her disappointment - not so vivid,
Neither is she livid,
As she walks through the metal doors to visit.
She sends them money as she sends up her prayers,
She sends out her letters to show that she cares.

What a beautiful strong woman as she grins & bears...
Because leaving is not an option,
Despite the lethal concoction of over-charging,
Over-sentencing & over-looking their innocence;
Oh, how they all use to be so innocent...
And though they may be guilty of certain crimes,
You can still hear her screaming, "He Still is mine!"

You can tell that she said it like she meant it.
She will never take a leave of absence
or a day off or stand down,
Unless they are dead & gone,
Or until they finally come home.
Life reveals many amazing facts
But there is one above any other;
We all wouldn't exist,
If it wasn't for a mother.

Mother's Day Is Everyday

Today I take great pleasure, as I reflect on a day of great significance. It's Mother's Day; where across the globe mothers are being celebrated for their exemplary action, attitude & attentiveness towards, not just their own children, but civilization as a whole. You see, she is always a mother, 24 hours of the day, seven days a week. She carries her mother title wherever she goes. In fact, she is a mother before she is even a mother, simply because she is a woman.

Women are created with the software of a mother already existing as they themselves are still a child. It is true; they are nurturers by design, they are compassionate in their nature and patient by patent. Their level of care for those around them supersedes that of a man by leaps & bounds. They see what we can't see, they sense what we can't feel and their love is the greatest force in the universe.

 Take a mother out of the home and it simply becomes a building occupied. When she is away at soccer practice, isn't she a mother to all, not just her own? What about at work as a nurse – her caring has no limit. She can work at a checkout stand in a grocery store and still offer you a gentle smile or a kind word. She has the unique ability to be the mother and father and grandmother all at once, all while being a pillar of her community. Who else will bake the cookies or cook at the community events? If a man should fall or scrape his knee, watch who will come to his aid. When he is down and out and feeling in despair, take notice of who will come to encourage him.

A mother not only carries the child she bares, but forever carries the world on her shoulders. No other God creation has overcome & evolved like a woman! She endured the most heinous violation of being raped by a slave master (that is for a black woman), but white women have suffered too; they all know so well the weight of a sexual assault, being pinned down... yet still they rise.

When the industrial work complex came to full bloom, they maintained the entire household, while husbands worked long days. She has always been more than just a mother; she had to be the cleaning lady, the chef, the taxi driver and she had to somehow be in the mood for loving on her husband after a long & exhaustive day. When the information age came and behind it technology boomed, she continued to be all she ever was and now leading in some of our largest companies around the globe. Women have grown by leaps & bounds, forging ahead as teachers, leaders, lawyers, doctors; from secretaries at Jiffy Lube, to Secretary of State, Presidents of Powerful Nations and among other 3 letter words like "CEO", she never relinquishes the one she will hold forever...
MOM

To All a Goodnight

I'm leaving now,
I'm on the next train,
I know it's going to hurt
and cause you all some pain.
But your lives must go on,
You have to maintain.
Your race is not over,
Even though mine is done;
Don't see my departure as a lost,
For I have won.
I've come in first place in a whole lot of hearts,
So many to count,
I don't know where to start.
We wake each day with an assignment to complete
and when we are done,
We lay for our final sleep.
I know you will weep and be taken by sorrow –
I'm gone today but you still have tomorrow.
You still have a race and I'll be watching you run it.
I know you can do it because I've already done it.
I'm headed to Glory,
It's going to be a long flight,
Until we see each other again...
To All a Good Night.

Infiniti

From the moment of conception, you were destined to win.
Brought into this word, back faced against the wind.
Your mother was a single parent – your daddy in the pen...
I wonder did you know?
Maybe that was why you were crying.
A new child was born while her parents were dying.
It was only because of you that we both kept on trying
You didn't even know,
But you were already inspiring.
Destined to win and so your journey began,
You were pushed to your limits at every single stage.
You were pushed, literally pushed
And still you kept on pushing...
You always managed to get past it all.
When others lost their battle, you didn't even fall.
Even when you were discouraged,
You still stood tall.
When I look back over your life I'm amazed at it all.
You took a negative and made it a positive
And you refused to be beat...
I wonder do you know how much you inspire me?
Now you're at a point where you turn another page-
You make so many proud
As you walk across the stage.
I'm eager to see what's next in your life-
I so believe in you, regardless of what you do
So remember these true words and always carry them within...
Infiniti Desiree Gray, You Were Born Destined to Win!

Love Words
Part 2

Karma

You think you found love on a 2 -Way street,
He's sweet, she's sweet, so happy to meet.
So you date and you court,
You get married never to divorce;
The force of gravitational pull,
This must be real,
Neither can deny how each other feels.
The love vibe is moving so you move in;
Together till death do you part;
Right at the moment is where trouble begins to start.
Complacency shows its nature.
She once was in love,
Slowly feeling like she hates you-
Like writings a bad line,
She now wishes she could erase you.
At first, no one could replace you;
Maybe that was before you were unfaithful.
She put it all on the table,
Yet you dealt from under the table...
A true love story now turned into a fable.
Contentment has created resentment
As you forget the vows once mentioned;
As if they were never said...
Somehow a love full of life is now being seen as dead.
Trying to outsmart love
Only to get caught in its web-
You betrayed her, it betrayed you,
You apologize, she refused to oblige...
What a facade.
You left a broken heart and dismantled love's trust,
Apparently forgetting what was written –
Karma, which is 10 times plus.

Love Contractions

Beautiful Butterfly,
Devine woman of the Universe,
Carrier of the greatest love ever.
Black & Sensational,
Your love is inspirational,
You have taken me high,
I did not know how,
But now I can fly.
Eyes wide open,
You've brought out everything in me,
Your love is so plenty –
Might I fill you up so you never go empty?
I'll be your love slave,
Go ahead and Pimp me...
I'm eager to work as a labor of love,
I'm eager to taste one more bite of your love.
The merging of our hearts has created these love sparks,
Thinking back on our love and when it had its first start.
Excited that I even know you,
Grateful to share our lives together,
Without a shadow of a doubt, you have made my life better.
I know things can get rough,
But they also can get better.
I know our love is right now...
But it's also forever.
Never in a doubt, never without a question,
Never will I forget how much you are a blessing.
My love for you is endless and it's only the beginning,
Our life has become a Fairytale...
With One Amazing Ending.

Your Fairytale King

When love is in effect, only the matter of heart is at play,
It's only you who brings out the best in me – selectively,
I have chosen you to love me or have you chosen me to love you?
It's all unsure yet so very pure.
I am tickled when you express any kind of affection my way.
It's the energy to my cord that lights my lamp... rather my heart.
You have my heart, so fragile yet full of life,
Like the beauty of an imported vase,
If not carefully handled it could end up in shattered pieces.
We must be careful, the delicate matter of love is in our hands,
Often taken for granted...
We must manage not to repeat the downfall of so many others.
Being true to ourselves as individuals & as lovers.
We have traveled into this gorgeous land of love
Expecting a wonderful sight to see,
Expressing our love so naturally-
Delighted in what we have come to be;
Exciting, I think we both can agree...
Surprising, I'm ready to get on one knee.
Take all my love, the ring is included.
My life was mundane but now you improved it,
My heart was on mute, it took you to unmute it,
Our love is volcanic, it can't be disputed.
I give you my promise, it can't be uprooted.
I'll give you my all... Nothing excluded.
My Fairytale Dream,
My Fairytale Queen,
Please hold onto these words...

Love,
Your Fairytale King!

Blessed For the Love I Found

You told me that you love me,
I felt it before you told me,
I knew it when you held me.
When we kissed it said hello,
When we touched...
I wanted it more.
As you perspired it escaped your pores.
I found it in your smile,
I watched it sparkle within your eyes,
I tasted it on your lips,
I felt it inside your thighs.
It was in every giggle and every laugh,
On every plate...
In every glass.
It's in your presence – it seems so vast,
The way you give it,
It makes me glad.
It's refreshing like a beautiful sunny day,
Soothing like an ice-cold shake.
My love senses lied dormant, but now they're wide awake-
Eager to participate...
Excited to exchange vows,
Thankful for the gift you gave,
Blessed for the love I found.

Our Love Is a Magical Place

Flowers in the dirt,
Love in the air,
The sun is shining bright,
People everywhere.

Butterflies flying,
Love birds singing,
Lost inside your love,
Gives new meaning.
This is where I'm at,
This is how I'm feeling,
Tired of holding my breath,
Now I'm finally breathing.
Stuck in one place,
Now I'm finally leaving.

I'm soaring like the birds,
Of course you are the reason,
Of course you're worth believing
and of course I'm never leaving.
Loving you every day,
Of course it's worth repeating.

A diamond in the rough,
A treasure in the sea,
You are more than it all...
At least you are to me.

Sweet Music

The melody moves through the blades of the grass,
Is it Rhythm & Blues, R&B or Jazz?
Life has put us on a path,
A journey we'll travel to the days of last.
My heart laughs,
That's how much your existence means.
That's how much joy & happiness you bring.
I'm ready to sing, whistle & skip,
To follow the path down the yellow brick road;
I'm off to see the wizard,
To tell him you're my pot of gold.
To tell the Leprechaun I don't need no lucky charm
Because all I ever wanted is already in my arms.
Put the Jeanie back in the bottle,
Tell him to stay planted;
Cuz the best wish I could imagine,
Has already been granted.
Take the Wishbone and the wishing well,
Give it to someone else and wish them well.
No need to find a Penny to find good luck
Because the day I found you was more than enough.

From The Big Man Above

Nothing was said, although the chemistry had spoken,
Although I was hoping that the silence would be broken.
A ball of emotions sat quietly still,
Every encounter... you could feel.
Tell me, how did it feel?
When did it come or how did you know...
What did you say, when it began to grow?
When I began to sow, did it titillate your senses?
Did you throw up your defenses or was it a general consensus?
That Heaven must have sent this,
That Heaven must have meant this;
This showery love mist that renders one defenseless...
because I am defenseless.
The switch of your hips hypnotizes my senses
but the essence of your soul takes me to a spiritual dimension.
You have my attention.
The silence is broken and surely I am listening.
My heart has spoken can you hear what it is whispering?
"I love you" is what it is speaking...
My question to you is what is yours speaking?
Has it not been weakened...
Or have you found what your heart has been seeking?
Just reach in and look in my chest,
See a genuine heart, then pray for the rest;
I know I'm not perfect but I'll give you my best...
I know I'm incarcerated but give me a chance,
and yes, it may be difficult but you won't regret it.
Because I'm betting on God and that's a safe bet.
I know a lot is at stake and things may have to wait
and if that be the case, then know that I'm okay...
But know there isn't a thing that can stop this Heavenly Love,
Especially when it all started...
From The Big Man Above.

Love Potion

Traveling at the speed of light,
Moving through the curves of life,
Trying to find the one that's right;
Looking for the perfect wife.
Never know till it comes to light –
If you let it go, it may come to bite,
So go with the flow and enjoy the flight.
Travel the seas of different emotions,
Stimulated by magic potion;
Ecstasy is just across the ocean,
Exotic lands in the mix of emotions –
Love's throttling,
You can feel every emotion,
Through the window pane you can see the convulsions –
It's a picture frame of volcanic explosions.
It can't be contained,
You can tell by the lava,
It's burning with flames...
An emotional saga.
Makes you wanna go faster,
Makes you wanna go harder –
You can smell the perfume
but it's not Estee Lauder.
Carefully hid,
It all came in a Trojan,
But the candles revealed... It was a True Love Potion.

True Love Stands

Expressions as they fall
Leaves an impression on the wall...
Encased you find words that speaks to us all.
That beats like a heart,
They release a Euphoric,
Leave you searching for the rose
in the middle of the forest...
Leaves you in the middle of nowhere without a tourist,
Takes you bungee jumping without the cord...
You travel the sky flying on your own wings;
You're lifted up high,
Sweet melody sings.
That's what love is,
That's what love brings...
That's how love feels,
That's what love means.
And if you just ask, it'll take you to a deep sweat,
If you close the curtain, it'll make you very wet...
If you don't know it,
Maybe it's time you two met.
I'm so glad that we met...
I'm so glad that we danced;
I'm so glad we romanced,
I'm so glad for this chance.
For you're my every woman...
Hope to be your every man,
True love takes you high-
but it also truly stands.

The Heart Speaks

Your love is tender, soft & warm.
Yearning for your soft kiss, I miss every beautiful thing about you –
Without you, my life would be so empty.
Yet it's plenty...
Filled with smiles, joy and adventure.
Like a roller coaster ride you take me high, then low, then high again;
I'm giddy for your love,
You got my head in a spin.
We're more than lovers, we're also friends...
Can't wait to see how it ends, only to begin again.
I love you...
It can never be enough and though we struggle at times
and though we fuss and argue,
I can never forget the day I first saw you.
So beautiful in your walk,
Your radiant face...
The melody of your talk.
I'm smiling thinking back on all we've shared,
Never in question that I care;
Protect your heart at all cost, is what I swear,
Just hang on tight, we're almost there...
and if you grow weak,
and your eyes leak-
Know that I got you, seven days of the week.
The way that I love you is more than I am,
More than I have ever given;
I'm finally living the American dream of love
and know without question,
It's from the big man above.
Let's fly together like two eagles in the sky;
Please baby, don't cry, let me dry your eyes.
Let me sing you songs that melt your heart to sleep,
Let me feel you breathe... let me feel your touch.
Let me know your love,
Let me,
Just please let me, be all you ever need...
Because you are all I ever want.

The Heart Listens

Your beauty is so ageless,
Your smile is so contagious;
Your love is outrageous...
I'm so glad God made this.
Your sparkles are so bright,
Even in the crowd of millions,
You touch me just right.
Creating the most wonderful feelings
You make me feel loved, not so easily done,
You captured my heart,
Yet, I feel like I won.
You're simply amazing
In who you are and all that you do...
You are definitely a star.
My supermodel chic,
My Victoria's Secret lady,
Can't wait to show the world,
"There goes my baby"

There goes my woman, there goes my wife
That's who I'll be loving for the rest of my life.
You're strong in love and soft in nature,
You're specially made,
Through God's creation.
I marvel your love and I will never get enough...
Forever we will be –
Through it all, no matter what!

So Beautiful and Clear

If the stars could talk, I'm sure they would say you're one of them.
If the moon light needed replacing,
I'm sure you would make a great replacement.
If the sun decided not to show up for work,
I'm sure you are the only person who can shine as bright & beautiful.
Who needs to witness a rainbow,
When all they have to do is witness you and your colorful personality?

I suppose it is great being you,
Given all the many wonderful things you are;
Your life is very inspirational.
Your love quite phenomenal and your smile simply contagious.
Imagining this world without you in it, I draw a blank-
Imagining this world with you in it and I see everything
So Beautiful & Clear

Questions

Have you ever watched the blades of grass wave as you walked by?
Ever wonder if those soaring eagles are looking down at you saying,
"Come Join Me"?
Have you ever walked past a beautiful flower bed and heard them say,
"Have a wonderful day"?
Have you ever considered on a hot sunny day
that the wind was blowing just for you?
That the birds chirping above were actually serenading you?
Have you ever seen a butterfly and thought you were looking in the mirror?
That beaches were made for your feet to walk on?
That every star in the sky is related to you?
That "Amazing" is not really a word, instead it's your name?
Could you ever imagine someone feeling this way about you?
Don't you think this would be a good time to start?

So Glad You Were Born

Every great thought in my mind begins with you.
Every time I see you or speak to you, I'm thinking "What a great feeling".
Every great place I go, every great experience I encounter,
All reminds me of the greatness in you.
Nothing compares to the smile you are able to paint on my face-
Even when I'm in a bad mood, it seems hard to erase...
You are hard to replace.
People who don't know our love find it hard to relate.
You are a beautiful flower and everyone stops to stare
I'm delighted to have you,
We make a wonderful pair;
Even when you're not around,
Your scent is in the air.
If everyone else was like you then you wouldn't be rare...
So special, so kind,
So gentle, so warm;
So thankful, so grateful...
So glad you were born.

Getting to Know Ricky Kidd

Ricky's passion for writing began when he was twelve years old. Starting with poetry and by age 15 he had written two short plays. Since then, Ricky has gone on to write a children's book, short and long plays, movie scripts, fiction, nonfiction and naturally, poetry. With Vivid Expressions, Ricky has begun to release pages of his passion and with so much more to come, he hopes his writings will positively impact people's lives.

Ricky's case has been picked up by the Midwest Innocent Project of UMKC. Together, many have joined the fight for Ricky's freedom. Including Kansas City Police Commissioner – Alvin Brooks, who believes strongly that the wrong person is in prison. Ricky's case has had write ups and features in the St. Louis American Newspaper, KSHB 41-Action News, The Kansas City Call Newspaper, The New York Daily News, The Popular News & Information website, Reddit, as well as 24 Media Network in Sweden.

To Learn More Visit:

- http://www.MIP.org
- http://www.FreeRickyKidd.com
- JusticeForRicky @ Facebook
- RickyKiddBooks@Facebook

Made in the USA
Middletown, DE
27 July 2020

13856587R00080